BE KIND TO YOUR MIND

BE KIND TO YOUR MIND

An Hachette UK Company
www.hachette.co.uk

Vie Books, an imprint of Summersdale Publishers Ltd
Part of Octopus Publishing Group Limited
Carmelite House
50 Victoria Embankment
LONDON
EC4Y 0DZ
UK

www.summersdale.com

Hachette Ireland
8 Castlecourt
Castleknock
Dublin 15
Ireland

www.hachettebooksireland.ie

Printed and bound in China

ISBN: 978-1-78783-256-5

Substantial discounts on bulk quantities of Summersdale books are available to corporations, professional associations and other organizations. For details contact general enquiries: telephone: +44 (0) 1243 771107 or email: enquiries@summersdale.com.

Printed on paper from sustainable resources

BE KIND TO YOUR MIND

A pocket guide to looking after your mental health

CLAIRE CHAMBERLAIN

VERY LITTLE IS NEEDED TO MAKE A HAPPY LIFE; IT IS ALL WITHIN YOURSELF, IN YOUR WAY OF THINKING.

MARCUS AURELIUS

CONTENTS

INTRODUCTION

In today's increasingly hectic world, it can be easy to overlook your own happiness and mental health, even if you don't mean to. But by taking steps to slow down, recharge and live more mindfully, it's perfectly possible to nurture your mind, body and spirit, so that any moments of worry become less frequent and more manageable. Throughout the following pages, you will find a series of tips that are designed to help improve your mental health and leave you feeling calm, positive and empowered. With chapters covering everything from mindfulness to gratitude, and with simple ideas that take a few seconds as well as those that require a bit more time, you will find something to suit you. One thing's for sure: by taking positive steps towards caring for your own mental health, you are on a journey to becoming happier, healthier and more resilient. Are you ready to be kinder to your mind? Then let's get started...

CALM YOUR MIND

Does it feel like you often race through the day, driven by stress? Are you harbouring unspoken worries, or do you regularly experience a sense of free-floating anxiety? If any of this sounds familiar, it's time to start addressing these issues to help you feel more resilient and better able to handle whatever life throws at you. Delving into the underlying causes of anxiety can seem daunting at first, but don't worry — it's unlikely that your whole mindset needs overhauling. You will probably find that by confronting previously unspoken worries and subtly shifting your outlook, you will vastly improve your mental health. In this chapter, we'll begin to address the issues of stress and anxiety, and look at a variety of ways you can boost your mental strength and calm your racing mind.

WHAT IS STRESS?

Stress is the feeling of being unable to cope in the face of pressure. This pressure can be either mental or emotional, and can stem from work, financial or relationship concerns, or any number of other life demands. While stress itself is not a mental health condition, it can cause serious mental issues, such as worry and anxiety. As stress releases hormones into the bloodstream that trigger the "fight, flight or freeze" response, it also causes a physical reaction, which can manifest as muscle tension, raised blood pressure and shallow breathing. What's more, feelings of helplessness that come from stress can be mentally draining. However, by taking measures to manage your stress, you can begin to deal with it effectively and proactively.

WORRYING DOESN'T STOP THE BAD STUFF FROM HAPPENING. IT JUST STOPS YOU FROM ENJOYING ALL THE GOOD STUFF.

KAREN SALMANSOHN

UNDERSTANDING ANXIETY

Anxiety is something that most people experience at some point. If you're about to start a new job, give a big presentation or do anything that pushes you outside of your comfort zone, it's likely you will be familiar with that nagging feeling of worry in the pit of your stomach. In instances like these, anxiety is entirely natural. It's only when it becomes a fairly constant presence in your life, and even starts to affect the way you live, that it gets more serious — for example, if your anxiety is constant, your fears are out of proportion, or you start avoiding certain situations because of your anxiety. There may also be physical symptoms, including muscle tension, nausea, butterflies in your stomach, headaches and dizziness. Being able to calm your mind is a powerful way to ease anxiety.

IDENTIFY YOUR TRIGGERS

To start dealing with stress and anxiety, begin paying attention to the circumstances that precede episodes. Is there a pattern? By spending a little time identifying your triggers, you'll be able to manage them more effectively. For example, you might notice you feel most anxious on days where you are overly tired, in which case getting to bed earlier each night may help.

DON'T BE PUSHED AROUND BY THE FEARS IN YOUR MIND. BE LED BY THE DREAMS IN YOUR HEART.

ROY T. BENNETT

CHALLENGE NEGATIVE THINKING

Don't simply accept negative thoughts — start reframing them in a more positive way. For example, telling yourself, "I'm not confident enough" right before a social event will disempower you. What could you say instead? Perhaps, "This situation has always made me nervous in the past, but I'm stronger than I give myself credit for. I can do this."

SEEK INNER SILENCE

Becoming aware of the silence between your thoughts can be wonderfully calming. Find a time when you can sit quietly for ten minutes and begin to notice your thoughts. Really listen to that voice inside your head. What's it saying? Don't judge your thoughts — simply become an observer. Then start to notice the silence in between each thought, however brief. Start focusing your attention on these silences, rather than the thoughts. Are the silences becoming longer? Do they feel more peaceful? Seeking out this silence in your mind is a powerful reminder that you can access the calm beneath your thoughts whenever you wish.

WITHIN YOU THERE IS A STILLNESS AND A SANCTUARY TO WHICH YOU CAN RETREAT AT ANY TIME AND BE YOURSELF.

HERMANN HESSE

SWITCH OFF

We live in an "always-on" world, where we feel we need to be up to date with the latest news and gossip every minute of every day via technology. But constantly checking our phones, sending messages, sharing photos and responding to alerts can become draining — and it's proven that it's not great for your mental health. Start building some "offline" time into your life each day — time when you don't have your phone to hand every moment. Switching off for even 20 minutes is a great start, or simply pop your phone on silent for a while. Why not instigate a phone amnesty in your home one day a week, where every member of the household leaves their phone off? You'll be amazed how much more connected you feel with those around you when you're not all staring at screens.

ASK FOR SUPPORT

When you start feeling overwhelmed, it's easy to believe that you have to do everything on your own. You don't. So take a deep breath and enlist some help. You will likely find that a loved one, friend or colleague will be happy to lend a hand. It can sometimes feel hard to reach out to others, especially if you've been bottling up worries and pressures — if you feel awkward asking face to face, a friendly email or text is a good option.

YOU MAY NOT CONTROL ALL THE EVENTS THAT HAPPEN TO YOU, BUT YOU CAN DECIDE NOT TO BE REDUCED BY THEM.

MAYA ANGELOU

TALK IT THROUGH

As the saying goes, a problem shared is a problem halved. Whatever is worrying or upsetting you is likely to feel far less threatening if you open up to someone close to you and let them know what's been going on. It can be scary telling someone you've been struggling, especially if you've put up a facade so that everyone thinks your life is rosy. But talking a problem through with someone who cares for you will lift the weight from your shoulders. Why not invite a friend out for a walk and open up to them? It will work wonders.

GIVE YOURSELF
A BREAK

Enjoying a moment to yourself
each day is the perfect way to
instil calm in your life. Even just five
minutes of peace can make a world of
difference. Sit in a garden and enjoy the
feeling of sunshine on your skin, try a
deep breathing exercise or savour
a cup of hot tea — the
choice is yours.

At the end of the day, remind yourself that you did the best you could today, and that is good enough.

LORI DESCHENE

LET GO OF PERFECTION

Odd as it may seem, "perfection" is not a healthy or realistic standard to aim for. Feeling that everything you do has to be flawless will not only disrupt your peace of mind, but will also stop you from ever trying anything new or challenging yourself, for fear that you might make a mistake. By all means aim to do your best, but never feel you have fallen short, especially if you have put all your effort into something. There is true peace to be found in being courageous enough to give something a go even though it may turn out less than perfect.

ONCE YOU CHOOSE HOPE, ANYTHING IS POSSIBLE.

CHRISTOPHER REEVE

REFRAME STRESS

Reframing stress can help you find the positives in challenging situations. For example, instead of asking, "Why is this happening to me?" ask, "What can I learn from this?" With a positive change of mindset, times of stress can actually spark personal insights and growth.

STOP COMPARING YOURSELF TO OTHERS

Your life is different from the lives of those around you. Wishing circumstances were different or comparing your life/situation/body to other people's will only result in you feeling bad about yourself. You are unique, beautiful and special — it's time to start celebrating you!

EMBRACE MINDFULNESS

It's easy to become so engrossed with our thoughts on a day-to-day basis that we begin to lose touch with the world around us and even with our own bodies. By living purely inside our heads, we get distracted from the present moment, or become governed by worries, fears or anxieties — often unconsciously. For example, how often have you finished a meal without really noticing the taste and texture of your food? How many times have you arrived at a destination without having noticed a single detail about the path you walked down? How many times have you got lost inside your own head, playing out past or imaginary scenarios, the only outcome being increased anxiety or frustration? We all do it — but when our minds wander off, it stops us truly appreciating the present moment. Practising mindfulness is a simple and effective way of redressing the balance, helping you to focus more clearly on the world around you, thereby taking your focus away from unhelpful mental patterns. The tips in this chapter will help to explain mindfulness and its place in your life.

WHAT IS MINDFULNESS?

Mindfulness is the act of becoming consciously aware of the present moment exactly as it is, without judgement. It's a way of reconnecting with yourself and your immediate surroundings, without worries or anxieties crowding your mind, all of which stop you experiencing the moment fully. Its origins are deeply rooted in Buddhist meditation practices, although the foundation of modern-day mindfulness is widely attributed to Jon Kabat-Zinn, who developed a mindfulness-based stress-reduction programme in the seventies.

THE IMPORTANCE OF NOW

While we can sometimes feel depressed or regretful about moments in our past, or anxious about upcoming events in the future, the only moment we ever truly have is right now — the present moment. Rooting ourselves more firmly in the "now" can help us to let go of worries and regrets, fears and anxieties to live fully in the moment, experiencing life more energetically and vibrantly.

THE PRESENT MOMENT IS FILLED WITH JOY AND HAPPINESS. IF YOU ARE ATTENTIVE, YOU WILL SEE IT.

THÍCH NHẤT HẠNH

GETTING STARTED

While living in the moment is a simple practice, it can take a little time to get used to, so don't be hard on yourself if you find your mind constantly wandering to other thoughts at first. It can be easier to start practising mindfulness at a time when you feel calm but alert. Begin to notice your surroundings, your bodily sensations and any feelings you may be experiencing. If you notice a thought arising that takes your mind away from "now", acknowledge it without judgement, then draw your attention back to the present moment. In time, mindfulness can help you become comfortable with difficult situations or times of stress — grounding yourself in the moment, and noticing that you are safe in the here and now, enables you to slow your thoughts and combat anxiety.

STARTING TO MEDITATE

Meditation can have a deeply calming effect on both your mind and body, leaving you with a greater sense of well-being and increased energy. Meditation is essentially focused attention, and it can help you block out unwanted mental "chatter", worries and anxiety. There are many different meditation techniques, but whichever you decide to try, aim to clear your mind of all other thoughts or emotions. If you notice thoughts creeping in, simply draw your mind back to the focus of your attention. Aim for just ten minutes daily to begin with — even a short session can make a big difference to your well-being. If you struggle to get started, search for some guided meditations online.

NOTICE THE LITTLE THINGS

Get into the habit of noticing the often
overlooked things in your immediate
environment — a flower growing through
a crack in the pavement; a reflection
in a puddle; steam rising off your
coffee. This is an easy way to bring your
mindfulness practice into everyday life,
and a wonderful way of finding beauty
in seemingly mundane situations.

When you take a flower in your hand and really look at it, it's your world for the moment.

GEORGIA O'KEEFFE

BREATHE MORE DEEPLY

Consciously taking a series of long, slow, deep breaths is a centuries-old technique used to help counteract feelings of stress and anxiety. It works by interrupting the sympathetic nervous system (which produces the body's "fight, flight or freeze" response), and instead triggers the parasympathetic nervous system, which invokes a sense of relaxation and calm. It's so simple and effective that you can do it anywhere. Each time you start to feel overwhelmed, anxious, nervous, tense or stressed, start inhaling deeply, from the pit of your stomach up to the top of your lungs, then exhale slowly and fully, relaxing your shoulders as you do so.

IF YOU WANT TO CONQUER THE ANXIETY OF LIFE, LIVE IN THE MOMENT, LIVE IN THE BREATH.

AMIT RAY

PERFORM A BODY SCAN

A body-scan meditation can help you become fully aware of your body in the present moment, leaving you feeling recharged and relaxed. To begin, sit or lie comfortably, loosening any tight clothing. Take a few deep breaths, then start to bring your awareness to your feet: pay attention to how they feel resting on the floor, whether they are warm or cool, and whether they feel tense or relaxed. The aim is not to judge or change, but simply to notice. Slowly move your awareness up your body, through your legs, buttocks, hips, pelvis, lower back, stomach, chest, upper back, shoulders, arms, hands, fingers, neck, jaw, cheeks, eyes, forehead and temples, scanning each body part in that moment. Bringing your awareness to your body, rather than to your thoughts, is very grounding and can instil a sense of peace.

TO BE IN THE MOMENT IS THE MIRACLE.

OSHO

COUNT TO TEN

Taking a moment to pause can
help to interrupt feelings of stress,
anxiety and panic. Take a deep breath
and slowly count to ten. It might only
be a brief respite, but in that short
moment you will give yourself a little
space and time to calm your mind and
counteract any negative sensations
you have been experiencing.

TRY MEDITATION IN MOTION

While we often think of meditation as being a "still" practice, many people find it easier to enter a meditative, focused state while performing slow, controlled movements. Yoga, t'ai chi and qigong are all deeply rooted in spiritual practices and are excellent examples of how to blend movement, breathing and meditation. Designed to help evoke a sense of calm, peace and stillness within, as well as creating balance in the body, these practices help to improve both your mental and physical strength and flexibility. You can practice all three of these disciplines in the comfort of your own home or garden with the help of guided online tutorials, but if you're a beginner, it's always a good idea to find a local class where a qualified practitioner will be able to support and encourage you.

MAKE TIME
FOR YOUR PRACTICE

Whether you've decided to add
meditation, mindfulness, yoga or
another spiritual practice to your
routine, it's important to dedicate time
to it regularly. The busyness of everyday
life can easily mean that new well-being
practices get brushed aside, if you let
them. Set aside time each day — you
can even write it down in your diary
— to help your practice become
part of your routine.

In the midst of movement and chaos, keep stillness inside of you.

DEEPAK CHOPRA

RELISH PEACE AND QUIET

Sitting quietly for a few moments each day can help you to recharge. If you find you have a few minutes to yourself, refrain from putting music on or checking your emails. Simply sit quietly, with your eyes gently closed if possible, and soak in a little silence.

BENEFITS OF MINDFULNESS

By consciously choosing to live your life more mindfully each and every day, you will begin to notice some powerful positive changes to your well-being. Mindfulness has been scientifically proven to lower blood pressure, alleviate gastrointestinal problems, reduce chronic pain, aid sleep and treat a number of mental health issues, including depression and anxiety disorders. What's more, proponents report a greater capacity to handle challenging life events and the ability to form more meaningful connections with others. So stick with your daily practice — what positive changes are you noticing?

THE REAL MEDITATION IS HOW YOU LIVE YOUR LIFE.

JON KABAT-ZINN

STAY POSITIVE

It's easy to think that positive people are simply lucky to have such a carefree, happy-go-lucky approach to life. But while some of us do have a tendency towards more pessimistic thoughts, it is perfectly possible for even the most negative among us to cultivate a more optimistic outlook. By actively seeking out the good in life and adopting a few positive rituals and routines, you will soon find yourself feeling brighter, lighter and more upbeat. What's more, with increased positivity comes great resilience, confidence and joy. You will soon find that even the smallest and most unexpected encounters and events can spark happiness, and you will naturally begin to experience a greater sense of mental well-being in your day-to-day life. The following pages are designed to help you explore the ways in which both internal mindset shifts and external actions can help to boost your positivity.

REALIZE POSITIVITY IS A CHOICE

It can be easy to spiral into a negative mindset if you're going through a tough time. But it's important to realize that viewing life through a more positive lens is a choice — and it's a choice everyone can make. This simple shift in perspective can transform your life for the better. Of course, it's not always easy, and it won't mean bad things will never happen. But by searching for the positives in every situation, however small, you'll slowly begin to cast aside any negative vibes in your life. One of the most important realizations you will make once you start choosing to be positive is that you are accountable for your own happiness. It's not out there, dependent on other situations, people and events — it's within you.

You complain about seeing thorny rose bushes; me, I rejoice... that thorns have roses.

ALPHONSE KARR

CREATE A POSITIVE MORNING ROUTINE

Starting each morning with positive actions and intentions can help to influence your mindset throughout the day. Try beginning each day with rituals and habits that boost your energy and make you feel happy. Setting your alarm 15 minutes early so you have time for a spot of sunrise yoga, using a citrus-scented soap in the shower (studies have shown that the smell of citrus fruits can boost mood and reduce stress), eating a nutritious protein-packed breakfast (such as poached eggs and spinach on wholemeal toast) drinking tea from your favourite mug, or setting yourself a positive intention for the day can all help to put a spring in your step and a smile on your face.

THIS IS A WONDERFUL DAY. I'VE NEVER SEEN THIS ONE BEFORE.

MAYA ANGELOU

TRY AFFIRMATIONS

Research has found it's easier to create positive change when you repeat daily affirmations. Pick a phrase that resonates with you and reflects the positive feelings you wish to embody, such as, "I choose to be happy," or "I am strong, capable and fearless." By repeating your chosen affirmation several times a day, you will start to identify with the words, which experts say can help to shift your outlook.

ALTER YOUR LANGUAGE

Switching your mindset from negative to positive can sometimes be as simple as changing the way you talk to yourself — and others. Start noticing your internal dialogue, as well as your conversations with those around you. What is your tone? Are you often down on yourself? Do you find yourself focusing on bad news or events? How could you change this? Phrases such as, "I bet I won't be able to do this" can be flipped to "This might be challenging, but I'll never know unless I try," or if you notice you're often the first to point out the negatives in any given situation ("I bet the train will be delayed, as usual"), focus on only pointing out the positives you notice instead ("I'm so grateful I got a seat today!"). You'll be surprised how quickly your perspective on life shifts.

ATTITUDE IS
A LITTLE THING
THAT MAKES A
BIG DIFFERENCE.

ZIG ZIGLAR

LOOK ON THE BRIGHT SIDE

Each day, make a point of noticing at least
five good things in your life. These can
be big (spending time with a cherished
friend) or tiny (stopping to appreciate the
flowers in the park). The more often you do
this, the more accustomed you'll become
to looking on the bright side of life.

ONCE YOU REPLACE NEGATIVE THOUGHTS WITH POSITIVE ONES, YOU'LL START HAVING POSITIVE RESULTS.

WILLIE NELSON

SURROUND YOURSELF
WITH OPTIMISTIC PEOPLE

Think about who your most positive friends and family members are. How do they make you feel? The chances are, they are encouraging and supportive, and you feel more energized and invigorated after spending time in their company. Maintaining a positive mindset is far easier when those around you are optimistic and supportive, so try to spend time with these people. And remember, your vibe attracts your tribe! By cultivating a more optimistic internal attitude and mindset, you'll find positive people will naturally begin to gravitate towards you, too.

TREAT YOURSELF

Feeling low? A little pick-me-up might brighten your mood. Treating yourself to a bunch of flowers, a cup of coffee or a new book are great options, but you don't have to spend money: a stroll in the sunshine or an early night count, too. What does your soul need?

SMİLE MORE

Even if you don't feel like
breaking into a cheesy grin,
smiling actually alters your brain
chemistry. A smile prompts the release
of the feel-good neurotransmitters
serotonin, dopamine and endorphins,
which lift your mood — even when
the smile is fake! So turning
that frown upside down might
begin to induce feelings of
happiness and positivity.

HAPPINESS IS A QUALITY OF THE SOUL... NOT A FUNCTION OF ONE'S MATERIAL CIRCUMSTANCES.

ARISTOTLE

HAVE A LAUGH

A good old belly laugh is
one of the best ways to boost
happiness and feelings of positivity.
In fact, research shows that laughing
triggers the release of endorphins,
your body's feel-good hormones.
Watching a comedy or listening
to a funny podcast are great
ways to get the giggles!

DO SOMETHING THAT SCARES YOU

Facing up to challenges that scare you is a powerful way of proving to yourself that you are capable of more than you think. First, bring to mind the things you've been putting off because of nerves or self-doubt — perhaps it's asking for a pay rise, initiating a challenging conversation or trying a new sport. Try to work out what it is specifically that makes you nervous, then think of ways you might overcome those things. Who could you enlist to help you? Could you enrol in lessons or a course? Try visualizing how you'll feel after you've accomplished the task. Even taking small steps is something to celebrate and be proud of and will help to boost your confidence and self-esteem.

CULTIVATE AN OPTIMISTIC MIND, USE YOUR IMAGINATION... DARE TO BELIEVE THAT YOU CAN MAKE POSSIBLE WHAT OTHERS THINK IS IMPOSSIBLE.

RODOLFO COSTA

LISTEN TO UPBEAT MUSIC

It's a scientific fact — listening to music
you love makes you happy! What's more,
a study has shown that actively engaging
with music by dancing or singing, correlates
with even higher levels of happiness.
So play your favourite tunes and dance
around your living room or bedroom
for a burst of feel-good positivity.

TAKE UP A NEW HOBBY

Learning a new skill can give you a great sense of purpose and help you feel more positive. What is it you'd really love to do? For your hobby to inspire you, it must be completely yours — not something you think a partner, friend or family member would like you to do. Think about your passions and interests, and then take steps to make it happen. If you'd like to do something creative, there are so many possibilities out there, from life drawing and pottery to woodwork and jewellery making. Look for taster sessions or beginner's courses in your chosen activity and get started!

LOOK AFTER YOURSELF

Introducing a spot of self-care into your daily routine is a fabulous way of nurturing your mental, physical and emotional well-being. Make looking after yourself a daily habit to ensure you carve out time for yourself each and every day. Even just a few short moments to yourself can do wonders for your mind, body and soul, especially if you are currently experiencing feelings of stress and anxiety, or if you spend the majority of your time caring for others. Your self-care needs will likely change on a day-to-day basis, depending on your time constraints and energy levels. For example, if you can manage to free up half an hour at the very start of the day, you might like to kick-start your morning with a power walk or dynamic yoga session. If, on the other hand, you are feeling drained after a stressful day, a cup of herbal tea enjoyed in the peace and quiet of your garden might do the trick. If you have the luxury of a whole hour or more to yourself, you could indulge in a long soak in a hot bath; other days, your self-care practice might simply involve taking a series of deep breaths. And remember, looking after yourself covers the essentials too, including eating nutritious food to keep your body healthy. Read on to discover more about self-care and how it can benefit your mental health.

WHAT IS SELF-CARE?

Sometimes, the term "self-care" can be misinterpreted as a phrase that implies self-indulgence, but in fact, rather than simply being a nice treat, self-care is actually a vital way of preserving your own health. It refers to any deliberate act you undertake that protects and nurtures your physical, mental, emotional and spiritual well-being, and encompasses a great number of practices, from eating healthily, drinking plenty of water and exercising, to becoming more mindful, embracing meditation and spending time in nature. And of course, the odd pampering session will do your soul the world of good, too! The overall aim of self-care is to help relieve stress and anxiety, while nourishing your body, mind and soul, so it's important to make time for it every day.

DITCH THE GUILT

You might feel bad about taking time out for yourself or indulging in some downtime. But remember, you cannot pour from an empty cup. If feelings of guilt arise, challenge them head on: list three reasons why taking time out for yourself in that particular moment will not only be beneficial for you, but also for those you will interact with later on in the day. You deserve the same level of care and attention that you give to others.

WE NEED TO DO A BETTER JOB OF PUTTING OURSELVES HIGHER ON OUR OWN "TO DO" LIST.

MICHELLE OBAMA

FITTING IN "ME TIME"

If you feel like you're being pulled in every direction and have demands being made on your time from work, family and social commitments, it's easy to demote yourself to the bottom of your "to do" list. But remember, you don't always need lots of time — even just five minutes after lunch for some deep breathing or a short walk counts. You can also set alerts on your phone to remind you to do small, simple acts, like drinking a glass of water every hour, or getting up from your chair and stretching for 60 seconds. However little time you have, make sure you take it and make the most of it — you'll be amazed at the positive impact it will begin to have in your life.

When you recover or discover something that nourishes your soul and brings joy, care enough about yourself to make room for it in your life.

JEAN SHINODA BOLEN

LEARN TO SAY NO

If you think that saying no when someone asks you a favour makes you a bad person, think again. Many of us worry that saying no can seem uncaring — but what if, by constantly saying yes to others, you start putting yourself under too much pressure, damaging your own mental health? Unfortunately, many of us take on additional tasks, chores, projects and responsibilities without pausing to consider how it will affect our well-being — but it's important not to become overwhelmed. "Thanks for asking, but I'm afraid I can't," is a kind but firm response. It's also fine to buy yourself time. Saying, "Let me check my diary and get back to you," will allow you to consider how the request will affect your own time and energy.

FOLLOW YOUR OWN STAR!

DANTE ALIGHIERI

TAKE A DEEP BREATH

If you ever feel overwhelmed, take a moment to slowly inhale fully and exhale deeply. While you do so, become aware of the rise and fall of your chest; of your lungs filling and then emptying of air — make that one breath your whole world for the moment. A single, conscious breath is the simplest form of self-care.

RELAX WITH A CUP OF TEA

People have relaxed over cups of tea for thousands of years — in fact, Zen Buddhist tea-drinking ceremonies were created with the sole aim of aiding meditation. Scientific research backs this up — tea drinking actually stimulates alpha brainwaves, which are associated with deep relaxation and enhanced clarity, and certain types of tea can also adjust serotonin and dopamine levels, making you feel happier. Black and green teas are brilliant, but there are so many more varieties out there to tempt your taste buds: peppermint can boost your mood, ginger is a good pick-me-up and chamomile is wonderfully calming. Making time in your day to relax with a cup of tea really is good for your mind and soul.

DRINK ENOUGH WATER

Being even slightly dehydrated can affect not just your physical but also your mental health. In fact, some studies have shown that dehydration can lead to an increase in feelings of fatigue and anxiety, as well as loss of concentration and lower mood. All of which means that drinking plenty of water each day is an easy and important way to look after yourself. Current guidelines state that drinking six to eight glasses of water is best for optimum health. If you're unsure whether you're dehydrated, the best way to test is to check the colour of your urine! It should be a pale straw colour. If it's any darker, simply reach for a glass of water. Flavour it with lemon, mint or cucumber, and remember that juices, teas, coffee and soup all count, too.

LEARNING TO LOVE YOURSELF IS LIKE LEARNING TO WALK — ESSENTIAL, LIFE-CHANGING AND THE ONLY WAY TO STAND TALL.

VIRONIKA TUGALEVA

CUT BACK ON ALCOHOL

Alcohol is a depressant, which can leave you feeling stressed, anxious, tired and less able to cope with daily life. While it's true it can initially induce feelings of relaxation, these are short-lived and will often be outweighed by the negative effects. Cutting back will help to boost your mental well-being.

FUEL YOUR BODY PROPERLY

Eating a balanced, healthy diet is a great step towards good overall health, and is a positive act of self-care that will benefit both your mind and body. Fuelling yourself correctly will lead to improved energy and mental function, and you'll also be doing yourself a big favour in the physical health department, lowering your risk of developing cardiovascular problems, diabetes, high cholesterol and certain cancers. Always avoid fad diets, instead aiming to eat enough protein (such as beans, pulses, nuts, fish, tofu and lean meat), carbohydrates (wholegrain bread and pasta, rice and starchy vegetables) and healthy fats (avocados, oily fish, nuts and olive oil), as well as lots of tasty vitamin-rich fruits and vegetables.

SELF-COMPASSION SOOTHES THE MIND LIKE A LOVING FRIEND WHO'S WILLING TO LISTEN.

CHRISTOPHER GERMER

CUT BACK ON
PROCESSED FOODS

Processed foods high in
sugar and trans fats are bad
for both your body and mental
health. Scientists think the blood
sugar fluctuations and inflammation
associated with eating too many
refined foods, such as pastries
and cakes, increases your risk of
depression, as well as leaving you
feeling sluggish. So cutting
back will make your
mind happy.

RELAX IN A
WARM BATH

Think soothing warm water,
your favourite essential oil, a few
candles, fluffy towels — you get
the picture. While self-care isn't just
about pampering, the chance to relax
your muscles and soothe your mind
can be a wonderfully welcome treat,
and an evening bath ticks both
boxes. So go on... soak away
the stresses of the day.

ALMOST EVERYTHING WILL WORK AGAIN IF YOU UNPLUG IT FOR A FEW MINUTES, INCLUDING YOU.

ANNE LAMOTT

GET MORE SLEEP

Sleep is an essential physiological process that helps to restore both your mind and body. If you aren't getting enough on a regular basis, chances are you will begin to feel fatigued, irritable, possibly anxious and less able to cope with stress. Show yourself some extra care by aiming for eight hours' sleep each night — this might mean getting into bed a little earlier each evening, but you'll be amazed at the difference it will make to your mood and energy levels. Spending time relaxing before bedtime will increase your chances of drifting into a peaceful sleep, as will avoiding the blue light emitted from electronic devices, such as your phone or tablet, in the hour before your head hits the pillow.

BE KIND

Spreading a little love, joy and kindness is a small but significant way to make the world a nicer place for everyone. These acts of kindness don't have to be grand gestures — simply smiling at a stranger, asking a friend if they're OK or making time for someone who you think might need a pick-me-up are all easy ways of helping to brighten the lives of those around you. And it goes without saying that making others feel happy is a sure-fire way of making yourself feel happier, too! Being kind to others is also a wonderful opportunity to reflect on all the good things in your own life. The more you look out for the good things, the more good things you will begin to notice, until you have created an abundance of gratitude. This chapter is dedicated to the small ways you can make those around you feel special, as well as looking at how you can begin to appreciate how very special your own life is, too.

BEING KIND MAKES YOU HAPPY!

Of course being kind to others makes them feel happy, but did you know it could have the same effect on you, too? It turns out that the warm glow you feel from being altruistic is very real: studies have shown that being kind to others can have a big impact on your own happiness and mental health, even helping to alleviate depression in some cases. It's thought this could be down to the fact that being kind to others gives you a sense of purpose, increases life satisfaction and can help to strengthen (and even widen) your social circle — another reason, if you needed one, to be kind.

TRUE FORGIVENESS IS
WHEN YOU CAN SAY,
"THANK YOU FOR
THAT EXPERIENCE."

OPRAH WINFREY

FORGİVE YOURSELF – AND OTHERS

Holding on to resentment is a sure-fire way to experience anger, unhappiness and mental unrest. Constantly berating yourself for your past mistakes, or holding a grudge against someone else, has no beneficial purpose — on the contrary, it can actually be highly damaging and draining to your health. It's important to accept that you — and those around you — are human, and humans make mistakes. It's time to gently accept this humanness by forgiving past behaviours and moving on. Of course, make sure you learn from past errors and don't repeat actions that have been harmful to both yourself and others, but don't hold on to them. Instead, seize this moment, right now: it is your fresh start.

GRATITUDE IS A POWERFUL CATALYST FOR HAPPINESS. IT'S THE SPARK THAT LIGHTS A FIRE OF JOY IN YOUR SOUL.

AMY COLLETTE

KEEP A GRATITUDE JOURNAL

According to psychological research, gratitude is consistently linked to feelings of happiness, contentment and a sense that what you have is enough. Keeping a gratitude journal is a fantastic way of documenting all the good things in your life and everything you have to be thankful for. At the end of each day, simply write down three (or more!) things that you have felt grateful for — try to think of different things each day. Some days, this will feel easy, especially if exciting or joyful events have happened, or if you have spent time with a loved one. Other days, you may have to look a little more closely. By keeping a journal, you will start seeking out things to feel grateful for so you can write them down, thereby actively creating an abundance of joy and happiness in your life.

THERE IS A CALMNESS TO A LIFE LIVED IN GRATITUDE, A QUIET JOY.

RALPH H. BLUM

PAY A COMPLIMENT

Make a point of paying someone a sincere compliment every day. It could be a person you know or a complete stranger, but by throwing a little unexpected kindness their way, you will likely brighten up their day — and you never know how much they might need to hear a friendly remark.

I GENUINELY BELIEVE THAT HAPPINESS IS CONTAGIOUS AND A SINGLE SMILE COULD CHANGE A PERSON'S WHOLE DAY.

EMILY COXHEAD

SAY THANK YOU

Thanking someone is the quickest and easiest way of showing them that you appreciate the help or support they have given you. However small the action, a quick "thank you" can go a long way — and it's even more effective coupled with a smile!

LEND A HELPİNG HAND

Does someone you know need
a little help? Offer your support.
From babysitting for a friend to
shopping for an elderly neighbour every
so often, little acts won't be forgotten
and can go a long way to showing
those around you that there's still a lot
of love and kindness in the world.

EXPECT NOTHING IN RETURN

The more kind and generous acts you start doing for others, the more likely you are to find others are happy to return the favour. But don't ask for anything in return when offering your help or your time. Expecting nothing in return is all part of the joy of helping others — just think how happy you would feel if you were the recipient of a small and unexpected act of kindness!

LOVE AND KINDNESS
ARE NEVER WASTED.
THEY ALWAYS MAKE
A DIFFERENCE.

BARBARA DE ANGELIS

BUY A FRIEND FLOWERS...

... or chocolates, or a little something you know they'll love, for no reason at all other than the fact they're your friend and you appreciate having them in your life. You don't even have to spend money. Sending them a cute or funny e-card lets them know you're thinking of them.

LEAVE A NOTE

What could be lovelier (or easier!) than leaving small, uplifting, positive notes dotted around your local community for strangers to read? Who knows — you could really give someone a boost if they've been feeling low, alone or anxious. All you need is some small pieces of paper or card, a pen and a spot of creativity! Think about the type of messages you might like to see when you're out and about. "You're amazing," "Never give up," or "Always be kind to yourself" are just a few small ideas to help get you started. Leave them stuck to the bus stop, inside the pages of a library book, in a shopping basket at the supermarket — anywhere you like! You will never know who sees them, but that's the beauty of this random act of kindness.

Do things for people not because of who they are or what they do in return, but because of who you are.

HAROLD S. KUSHNER

CALL A FRIEND

All too often, the busyness of life gets in the way of making time for friends and family. Is there a loved one you haven't spoken to in a long time? Set aside time to pick up the phone and speak to them. Messages and emails are fine, but there's something about hearing a loved one's voice that sparks joy.

VOLUNTEER YOUR TIME

Giving up a little of your time is a fantastic way to give something back to the world. Plus, it's brilliant for your own well-being, too. In fact, according to research, volunteering can reduce stress levels, boost your confidence and self-esteem, give a sense of meaning to your life, improve social interaction, hone your skills and even lower your blood pressure, all while extending a spot of kindness to those around you. Not sure how to get started? Think about activities you enjoy or causes that mean a lot to you. What skills could you offer? Local schools, dementia cafés or community groups are a great place to start. Or you could think bigger — there are a whole host of opportunities to volunteer abroad if you have more time and a sense of adventure.

HUG A LOVED ONE

Oxytocin — the feel-good chemical in our bodies — is sometimes referred to as the "cuddle hormone"... and with good reason! The level of oxytocin in our bodies becomes elevated when we have physical contact with someone we care about, and this in turn makes us feel happier and reduces stress. Some studies have even shown it can reduce pain, boost immunity and lower blood pressure. So hugging doesn't just show someone you care — that hug is packed with a host of brilliant benefits for both of you. Go on... give someone you love a cuddle and put a smile on their face!

BALANCE YOUR LIFE

We hear so often that we should aim for a balanced life — but what does this mean exactly? We can probably all recall times when we have felt distinctly out of balance — times when we are overwhelmed, run down, frustrated and pulled too much in one particular direction, perhaps if our workload gets too big or our responsibilities within the family increase dramatically. We know we're experiencing balance, on the other hand, when we feel grounded, calm, energized and able to dedicate time to all the things that matter to us — including our own mental and physical well-being. When aiming for more balance, it can be helpful to think of all the elements of your life as separated into two categories: internal and external. The internal elements are things such as your physical and mental health, spirituality and meaningful connection with others. External elements include things like work, socializing and family commitments. To ensure you feel grounded, satisfied and balanced, it's important to ensure all these needs are met to a degree that feels right for you. The following tips are designed to help you create a little more space and harmony in your life, so that you have more time to dedicate to the things that matter most to you.

WHAT DOES "BALANCE" LOOK LIKE?

"Balance" will look different for everyone, depending on likes, dislikes, energy levels and personality, among other factors. But essentially, living a life that's in balance means creating harmony between all the various aspects of your life — your physical and mental needs, your work and responsibilities, your social life, and your passions and hobbies. Life and circumstances are ever-changing, so to achieve balance you might find you have to constantly reassess your priorities. For example, if you have a big work project on the go, you might need to skip a night out in favour of a yoga class or an early night, in order to regain balance.

YOU CAN DO ANYTHING, BUT NOT EVERYTHING.

DAVID ALLEN

SET YOURSELF GOALS

Setting goals is a brilliant way of figuring out what you want to achieve in life and then mapping out how (and when) you will get there. Goals are also a good way of helping you realize where you might be spending time doing things that are not important to you, allowing you to free up your energy for the people and things that really matter. Writing down your goals can help to solidify them in your mind. Long-term goals are great, as they can help to shape the course of your life, but make sure they are not so far into the future that you lose sight of them. Then set out some shorter-term goals that will help you achieve your end goals. Refer back to your list of goals regularly, for assurance and motivation.

WRITE A "TO DO" LIST

A daily or weekly "to do" list is a simple way
of freeing up your short-term memory, helping
you to feel calmer and in control. Seeing
tasks written down can make them seem
more manageable and being able to cross
each one off your list once it's completed
will help you feel capable and empowered.

You're only here for a short visit. Don't hurry, don't worry. And be sure to smell the flowers along the way.

WALTER HAGEN

STAY FLEXIBLE

While it's important to have goals,
remaining flexible in day-to-day life
rather than feeling you must adhere
to "rules" you have set yourself is one
of the keys to happiness. Be gentle with
yourself and others, and keep plans
flexible. Circumstances are constantly
changing, so try to go with the flow.

BE SPECIFIC ABOUT YOUR NEEDS

Knowing exactly the changes you need to make in your life in order to achieve more balance is important, so be specific. Telling yourself that you "just need a bit of time for yourself" is a vague statement that you may very well push aside when life gets hectic. Signing up for a weekly yoga class and vowing to go to bed half an hour earlier on week nights, on the other hand, is a more specific plan of action that you can stay accountable to.

LEARN TO PRIORITIZE

You can't do everything —
you're only human, and a big
part of achieving a more balanced
life is accepting this fact. If you start
feeling overwhelmed, list all your
responsibilities, then prioritize them.
Put your time and energy first
into the things that are
top of your list.

The thing that is really hard, and really amazing, is giving up on being perfect and beginning the work of becoming yourself.

ANNA QUINDLEN

CUT BACK ON COMMITMENTS

Are you being pulled in too many directions? Are there certain chores or commitments you could streamline, delegate or simply stop doing? Think about what's really important to you — it's OK to cut back on the things in your life that are not serving a purpose or bringing joy.

You don't always need to be getting stuff done. Sometimes it's perfectly OK, and absolutely necessary, to shut down, kick back, and do nothing.

LORI DESCHENE

DECLUTTER YOUR LIVING SPACE

Being constantly confronted with cluttered surfaces and cramped cupboards within your home is a sure-fire path to stress. Getting rid of unwanted items can be highly cathartic, ultimately leaving you with a more minimalistic living space that will help to promote a sense of peace and balance. Getting started can sometimes seem overwhelming, so it's a good idea to break the process down to make it more manageable. Start decluttering just one cupboard, or even just one drawer. Work through a new area of your home every chance you get — you'll be surprised how quickly it will add up! Rather than chucking everything into the bin, decide what can be recycled, donated to charity or given to a local refuge.

PUT YOURSELF FIRST SOMETIMES

Putting yourself first on the odd occasion does not make you a selfish person; it makes you a person who understands the importance of good mental health. Speak to friends or family members so they truly understand why you need time to recharge, and make arrangements to ensure it happens.

THINK BEFORE YOU BUY

Shopping can quickly become a habit, and before you know it you can easily fall into the trap of equating "more stuff" with happiness. In reality, studies show that while there is a temporary high from a spot of retail therapy, it only lasts for a few days, leaving you feeling lacking once more and in need of another shopping fix. The truth is that consumerism does not equal contentment. Instead, try embracing the idea of slow fashion: of reducing, reusing and repurposing; of mending what you already have; and of only buying what you truly need. This more conscious attitude towards shopping is profoundly more rewarding and will help keep unnecessary clutter out of your life.

FREEDOM FROM DESIRE LEADS TO INNER PEACE.

LAO TZU

ADDRESS YOUR FINANCES

It's hard to achieve balance in your life if you're harbouring financial fears, but it's a sad fact that money worries are a leading cause of anxiety. Seek advice on how to manage your money, prioritize your outgoings, and start paying off just one debt. It's a small step, but taking small steps can bring a sense of relief, and will help you to feel in control once more.

EARLY BIRD OR NIGHT OWL?

Start paying attention to your energy peaks and troughs throughout the day, then use them strategically. If you are a morning person, schedule meetings or tasks that require a high level of concentration before midday. Perhaps you could get up early to squeeze in an extra hour of work, or perform your high-intensity workout at sunrise. This will leave you time in the evening to relax, unwind and get an early night. If you're more of an evening person, start the day with some gentle stretching, leave harder tasks until late afternoon or evening when you're at your peak, and save fitness classes for after work. Living more in alignment with your own energy rhythms will help you get the most out of each day and make it easier to achieve balance.

For fast-acting relief, try slowing down.

JANE WAGNER

STEP OUTDOORS

Numerous studies have found that spending time in the natural world elevates your well-being — so much so, in fact, that many doctors now advise spending time in nature as "ecotherapy" to help improve mental health. The great outdoors is proven to help alleviate stress and anxiety, and research has shown that those who spend more time surrounded by nature experience improvements in mood, self-esteem, confidence and physical health. But while it's reassuring to learn that science backs it up, you probably know this for yourself already.

From wandering through woodland or listening to the gentle babbling of a river, to sitting in a garden or strolling barefoot on the grass, we all know that time spent in nature is a soothing balm for the mind and soul. The following tips are filled with inspiring ideas — both big and small — to help you deepen your connection with Mother Nature and experience everyday outdoor wonders that will help to make your heart and mind happy.

STEP OUTSIDE

If you're feeling anxious or stressed, the simplest quick fix is to head outside, close your eyes and breathe in the fresh air. This can instantly help you feel more centred and grounded. Just a few minutes in the open air can give you the headspace you need to calm your mind and collect your thoughts.

ALLOW NATURE
TO TEACH YOU
STILLNESS.

ECKHART TOLLE

GET SOME SUNSHINE

Natural sunlight is a wonderful mood booster — and it's important for your health, too. Vitamin D (produced by your body when your skin is exposed to the sun) helps to maintain healthy bones, teeth and muscles, and scientists also believe there's a link between vitamin D and your mental health, with decreased levels of the vitamin associated with low mood and even seasonal affective disorder (SAD). So get outside as often as you can and soak up some "happy" rays! In winter months, when the sun can be too low in the sky for your body to make adequate levels of vitamin D, a food supplement can be beneficial.

TRY FOREST BATHING

The Japanese tradition of *shinrin-yoku,* which translates as "forest bathing", is beginning to be adopted by Western cultures as a means of improving mental health and evoking a sense of inner peacefulness. The practice involves simply spending time walking slowly through or sitting in a woodland or forest, "bathing" in the green space and allowing your body and mind to reconnect with the natural world. Immersing yourself in nature in this way is a wonderfully holistic way of calming your mind, reducing stress levels, improving your mood and enhancing creativity. Even a short amount of time spent in green space is good for your soul, so for enhanced mental wellness soak up a little nature whenever you get the chance.

ADOPT THE PACE OF NATURE: HER SECRET IS PATIENCE.

RALPH WALDO EMERSON

FORGET NOT THAT THE EARTH DELIGHTS TO FEEL YOUR BARE FEET AND THE WINDS LONG TO PLAY WITH YOUR HAIR.

KAHLIL GIBRAN

GET IN TOUCH
WITH THE EARTH

Spending a little time barefoot each day can be very grounding. Try going barefoot each time you stand in your garden, or when you visit a park or beach. Visualize yourself connecting with the earth, pay attention to the feel of soil, grass or sand beneath your feet, and imagine any stress seeping away through your bare soles.

GO FOR A WALK

Stepping outside and heading for a walk can do wonders for your mental health. In fact, research has shown that regular walking can boost both your mood and self-esteem, as well as reducing stress levels and easing fatigue, anxiety and depression. A stroll really is good for your soul.

MOVE MORE EVERY DAY

Moving your body more each day can go a long way to improving both your physical fitness and mental well-being. Walking instead of driving, getting off the bus a stop early, going for a walk in your lunch break or taking a longer route when out and about are easy ways to get more steps in each day.

BIG FITNESS GOAL? START SMALL

While you might have dreams of hiking up mountains, running marathons or cycling across continents, it's important to start small, especially if you haven't done much physical activity in a while. Of course, taking on challenges can be wonderful for your mental health, but only if you have built towards your goals gradually, increasing your physical fitness and mental resilience one step at a time. If you have an inspiring fitness goal you'd like to achieve, the first step is to break it down into smaller, achievable targets. For example, if you dream of running a marathon but are not yet a regular runner, download a beginner's walk/run programme, then enter a 5K event and build from there. Remember to celebrate each small step you take to fully appreciate the strides your body is taking.

IN EVERY WALK WITH
NATURE ONE RECEIVES FAR
MORE THAN HE SEEKS.

JOHN MUIR

WILDERNESS IS NOT A LUXURY BUT A NECESSITY OF THE HUMAN SPIRIT.

EDWARD ABBEY

GROW YOUR OWN

Growing your own vegetables, fruit or flowers is wonderfully rewarding — and it's not just the end product that brings joy. Nurturing seeds or young plants gives a sense of purpose and responsibility, and the sheer physical nature of gardening, coupled with the fact it brings you back in touch with nature in a very visceral way, can be a fantastically mindful occupation, taking your thoughts away from worries or anxieties and instead grounding you in the present moment. New to gardening? There's lots of help to be found online or in books to get you started, or head to your local garden centre for some support and advice. Even if you're lacking in outdoor space, you can easily grow herbs or salad leaves in pots on balconies or windowsills.

GET YOUR HEART RACING

Outdoor exercise is a wonderful way to boost your physical and mental health. Exercise is also proven to help reduce stress and anxiety, and to boost feelings of confidence, resilience, self-esteem and happiness by flooding your body with endorphins (the "happy hormones") and proving just how much you are capable of — which is often more than you realize. Whether you choose walking, running, cycling, wild swimming or something else, it's important to get your heart racing when you exercise to reap the maximum benefits. This means including regular intervals where you move at a faster pace. It can feel challenging at the time, but you'll feel fantastic after each exercise session!

BRING THE OUTSIDE IN

A few houseplants can brighten up any indoor space and are a fantastic way to bring the feel of the outdoors in. Certain houseplants, such as the peace lily, snake plant and English ivy, help to improve indoor air quality and rid your home of toxins as well as boosting your mental health, so there are a host of powerful benefits.

TRY WILD SWIMMING
(OR EVEN JUST DIP YOUR FEET!)

Research has proven what many wild swimmers already know to be true: that taking a dip in a natural body of water, such as a lake, river or sea is good for your mind, body and soul. It connects you instantly with nature, helps to calm your mind and promotes feelings of joy and happiness. What's more, the cold water also increases blood flow to your brain and core to help keep you warm — a side effect of which is often a boost in mood. Even a quick paddle will do the world of good. To ensure your safety, do your research first — check that water is safe to swim in, take measures to protect against hypothermia (such as wearing a wetsuit) if swimming in cold water and don't go wild swimming alone.

LOOK UP AT THE STARS

Gazing at the night sky can help put personal problems into perspective, as you take a moment to appreciate the beauty and sheer expanse of the galaxy. Stargazing can naturally help us slow down and mentally move beyond the busyness of everyday life, as well as sparking wonder and curiosity. On a clear night, pick a spot with low light pollution if possible, and lose yourself in the wonders of the night sky.

You are the sky. Everything else — it's just the weather.

PEMA CHÖDRÖN

CONCLUSION

After reading all the tips, ideas and quotes in this book, hopefully you feel motivated and inspired to take good care of your own mental well-being. By putting these suggestions into practice, you'll soon find yourself feeling refreshed, rejuvenated and more resilient — and your brighter mood will likely inspire others, too. Whenever you're feeling a bit low or overwhelmed by life's challenges, dip back into these pages and draw encouragement from the fact that boosting your mental health isn't a gigantic, daunting task: often, it simply requires you to take small steps, one at a time. Each little action you take will add up to a happier, healthier, more balanced you. So choose whichever tips appeal to you most and create your own daily ritual, or perhaps open the book at random for a surprise daily dose of positivity. However you choose to take the suggestions on board, this book is here for you whenever you need a little helping hand — and as a reminder to be kind to your mind.

If one's mind has peace, the whole world will appear peaceful.

RAMANA MAHARSHI

NOTES

If you're interested in finding out more about our books, find us on Facebook at **Summersdale Publishers** and follow us on Twitter at **@Summersdale**.

www.summersdale.com

IMAGE CREDITS